Original title:
Bananas and Blue Skies

Copyright © 2025 Creative Arts Management OÜ
All rights reserved.

Author: Maya Livingston
ISBN HARDBACK: 978-1-80586-398-4
ISBN PAPERBACK: 978-1-80586-870-5

Swaying in the Afternoon Glow

In the warm sun, we take our stance,
Chasing fruit that makes us dance.
Yellow dots in the fluffy trees,
Swinging with laughter, riding the breeze.

With each peel, a giggle escapes,
As we dodge the silly shapes.
Nature's candy, oh what a treat,
Every bite brings joy, can't be beat.

The Fruit That Lifts Our Spirits

Round and bright, a cheerful sight,
In our hands, they feel just right.
Bounces of laughter in every bite,
Sweetness beams in morning light.

They make us grin, they make us sing,
Oh, what joy this fruit can bring.
Add a twist, a sprinkle of fun,
Life's a party when we're done!

A Golden Horizon Awaits

Far beyond where the sun does set,
A treasure glows, we won't forget.
Peeking out from leafy greens,
Chasing dreams in fruity scenes.

With giggles loud and voices bright,
We gather 'round, hearts feel light.
Secrets shared from tree to tree,
As golden treats set our minds free.

Laughter Among the Canopies

In the green maze, we run and play,
Joyful shouts, we greet the day.
Hang on tight to the swinging vine,
Where mischief waits and smiles align.

Under the leaves, we tumble and roll,
With every slip, we're on a stroll.
Nature's jesters with a silly flair,
We find our fun hiding everywhere.

Soaring High Over Fields of Gold

In the orchard, birds take flight,
Jumping jays in pure delight.
Lemon hats and froggy croaks,
Giggling folks, and silly jokes.

Clouds like marshmallows drift by,
Tickled tongues, we laugh and sigh.
Bouncing on the golden ground,
Joyful leaps and silly sounds.

A Symphony of Yellow and Blue

Harmonies of sunny cheer,
A wobbly dance that draws us near.
Mirthful mocktails, sips and spills,
Bright balloons and rolling hills.

Crazy hats that wobble high,
Chasing dreams and butterflies.
Whispers sweet like candy rain,
Laughter echoing in the plain.

Mellow Days in Warm Embrace

In fields where laughter freely flows,
Tickled toes in sunshine glows.
Wrinkled smiles in cozy shade,
Every worry starts to fade.

Sunny splashes, playful squeals,
Silly stories, joking reels.
Napping beneath a leafy tree,
Dreaming of pure jubilee.

Daydreams of Sweetness and Sky

Giggles dance on the summer air,
Silly hats and messy hair.
Candy clouds in a sugary race,
Sunshine painted on every face.

Daydreams hop on marshmallow trails,
Jellybean boats with jelly sails.
In this land of whimsy free,
We're the stars of our own spree.

Joy in the Fruit Bowl

In the bowl, a twist of cheer,
Fruits are giggling, oh so near.
Yellow smiles, they laugh and play,
Dancing lightly, come what may.

With every bite, a silly sound,
Juicy joy is found all around.
Slice the laughter, share a grin,
Fruitful fun, let the games begin!

Harvest of Light and Laughter

Citrus rays in sunshine bright,
Happiness spills, pure delight.
A fruity party in my hand,
Jokes and jests, all unplanned.

Yellow peels, they wave hello,
Making bright the garden show.
With every munch, a burst of glee,
This fruity fun is wild and free!

Serenity in the Shade of Yellow

Underneath the leafy veil,
Fruits conspire, they tell a tale.
Whispers sweet in sunlit air,
Cheeky giggles, everywhere!

Nature's laughter softly sings,
As joy unfolds on leafy wings.
In the shade, we share a laugh,
Fruity tales that make us gasp.

Breezy Days and Golden Delights

Golden breezes swirl and sway,
Cheerful munches save the day.
Each slice brings a chuckled cheer,
Sunny moments, drawing near.

Tickled taste buds, smiles abound,
Fruits of laughter, joy profound.
Life is sweet, a silly dance,
Grab a piece, join the prance!

Citrus Glow and Daydreaming Skies

In a world where peels chat,
And yellow fruit wears a hat,
Laughter echoes in the breeze,
As we share our fruity tease.

With a twirl and joyful leap,
We make promises to keep,
Jumping high with silly glee,
Fruity dreams, oh let them be!

Nature's Lullaby in a Bright Embrace

Under a sun that radiates,
Silly tales of fruity fates,
Leaves whispering rhymes so sweet,
With giggles filling every street.

The ground is ripe with playful cheer,
Jokes unfold as friends draw near,
In this garden, laughter blooms,
As nature's laughter fills the rooms.

Vibrant Eden Under Endless Expanse

A landscape alive with zest,
Fruity frolics never rest,
Squirrels dance with crazy flair,
As we wander without a care.

The sun dips low, a golden smile,
Each moment lasts a joyful while,
In this realm where whimsy thrives,
We find joy in all our jives.

Sweetness Unfurled in the Day's Embrace

With each bite, a giggle's sound,
Jokes and laughter swirl around,
In this slice of sunny fun,
Every day feels like a run.

Sunkissed cheeks in playful light,
We chase shadows, full of might,
Laughter mingles in the air,
As we float without a care.

A Spectrum of Delight and Light

In a world so bright and loud,
Yellow fruits make me so proud.
Bouncing high with glee and cheer,
We twirl and laugh when they are near.

Silly hats and dancing feet,
Every corner feels so sweet.
With every twist and every sway,
Our joyous hearts will lead the way.

Embracing the Lure of Juicy Joy

A twisty tree with leafy crowns,
Delightful snacks in sunny towns.
We giggle at the tasty mess,
Oh, what fun! We must confess.

Puppies prance, and monkeys play,
Laughing in the golden ray.
Each bite brings a burst of fun,
We'll share this joy with everyone.

The Colors of Abundant Bliss

In gardens where the laughter sings,
A chubby critter finds his flings.
With stinky socks and funny hats,
We swing along with silly chats.

Bright and zany, here we go,
Wiggly worms put on a show.
With polka dots and stripes galore,
We celebrate the tasty core.

Graceful Dances of the Day

In a whimsical parade so wild,
A yellow fruit with a big smile.
Swirling skirts and lofty dreams,
We dance in playful, joyful streams.

Laughter echoes, joy abounds,
We spin and prance on silly grounds.
With every nibble shared in cheer,
We spread the fun for all to hear.

Cloudwatching Through Golden Glimmers

Fluffy shapes dance in the air,
A whale swims by without a care.
Underneath, we giggle and grin,
As cotton candy clouds begin to spin.

Waving wings of a bright butterfly,
A squirrel tells jokes from way up high.
We lay on grass, feeling quite free,
At this circus of shapes, come join me!

Sunkissed Moments of Delight

Sunbeams tickle our toes and feet,
As ants march by in a tiny fleet.
We dodge raindrops that never fall,
While trying to catch a bouncing ball.

Laughter bubbles like fizzy soda,
Each moment shines like a sweet goldenoda.
We chase shadows that run away,
In this playful dance of the day!

The Blissful Aura of Pure Nature

Daisies nodding in the gentle breeze,
Are gossiping trees among the leaves.
We sing with birds, an off-tune choir,
As giggles rise like smoke from a fire.

With a skip, we leap over puddles wide,
In this joyful rush, we take in the ride.
A friendly bee gives us quite a buzz,
While we hunt for treasure, just because!

An Ode to Warmth and Sweetness

With honey drips and sweetened hearts,
We share our dreams and silly parts.
Frogs jump high with a croak and a splash,
While we ponder how fast they can dash.

Giggles bubble like lemonade,
We bask in sunshine, completely unmade.
As warmth wraps us in a cozy hug,
We dance freely, giving the grass a tug!

The Sweetness of Sunlight and Softness of Clouds

In the garden of giggles, a fruit so bright,
Tickles the taste buds, a pure delight.
Sunbeams dance lightly, weaving their charm,
While whimsical breezes keep us warm.

Oh, fuzzy fellows, with laughter they burst,
Swinging and swaying, an anarchist's thirst.
Jokes grow in clusters, they dangle so free,
Each chuckle we gather, as sweet as can be.

Ripe Fruits Against a Sea of Serenity

Juicy jests hang low, like stars they gleam,
Mirthful moments float in a sunbeam's dream.
With every nibble, a giggle escapes,
As joy ripens softly, in nature's landscapes.

Amidst the green vines, a carnival brew,
A taste of the silly, in every hue.
High-flying fun, on a breeze it sails,
While laughter unravels in ticklish trails.

Joyful Yellow in a Canvas of Bliss

Sketches of sunlight on a canvas so wide,
Where laughter and flavors in harmony glide.
Cheeky delights, with skins wrapped in cheer,
Bring smiles to faces, from ear to ear.

Frolicsome fruits tease with each playful bite,
Chasing imaginations that take to flight.
In giggles we gather like clouds up above,
Creating a masterpiece, stitched with love.

Laughter in the Orchard and Lush Above

In orchards of whimsy, where silliness thrives,
Giggling fruits whisper, as laughter arrives.
Cheesy puns dangle like treasures untold,
In this land of vibrant, where joy is bold.

Swinging on branches, the humor takes flight,
Each pluck brings a fit of infectious delight.
Hands reaching up high, we tickle the sky,
In this fruity parade, we let worries fly.

Sweetness Spun in the Sky

In a world of yellow cheer,
Fruit dances near, no fear.
The clouds chuckle, full of glee,
As happy birds sing by the tree.

With every peel, a giggle flows,
Slick mischief where the laughter goes.
A slip and slide on sunny days,
Where joy's a game, and fun decays.

The sun beams down, a playful tease,
Making nature's laughter seize.
Bouncing fruits, they leap and twirl,
A celestial circus, a fruity whirl.

So grab a snack, do not delay,
Join the frolic, come what may.
In this bright realm of absurd delight,
Every moment's a comical flight.

Harmony in Bright Abundance

In patches bright, the laughter grows,
With critters clad in silly clothes.
A feast of colors fills the air,
Joy spreads wide, without a care.

Tiny creatures join the fun,
As sunshine smiles, oh, what a pun!
With every bite, the sweetness flows,
Bright hearts dance as the circus grows.

Around the bend, some squirrels prance,
Twisting their tails, they're in a trance.
They claim the crown of silly jest,
Nature's jesters, they do their best.

Have a laugh, let giggles rise,
In this land where humor flies.
Together we'll sing a merry tune,
In joyous echoes beneath the moon.

Adventures Amidst the Splendor

A twisty path through groves so bright,
With yellow shapes bringing delight.
Curious critters keep the score,
As playful antics ask for more.

Dancing vines, a wild parade,
In this wacky, sunny escapade.
Laughter peeks behind each leaf,
While mischief brings the wild relief.

Silly hats worn askew on heads,
Frolicking friends, no one dreads.
The air's electric, full of jest,
In every nook, there's joy expressed.

So heed the call of whirling fun,
In this vivid world, we all are one.
Let laughter reign, and spirits soar,
Adventures await, who could want more?

A Dance of Sweetness and Infinity

In a yellow suit, they sway and spin,
Wiggling to a tune, it's where you begin.
With every step, joy spreads!
Their giggles chatter, nature's thread.

Little fruits doing a jig, so divine,
Bouncing around like they own the line.
A twist and a turn, don't break a peel,
With laughter, they dance, it's all too surreal.

The Lightness of Summer's Bounty

A picnic spread under a sunny array,
Fruits in a frenzy, come out to play.
Slipping and sliding, they roll with glee,
    Chasing each other, a wild jubilee.

The breeze is a dancer, twirling around,
As laughter erupts from the grass-covered ground.
With every bright twist and zany cheer,
    They tumble in heaps, no room for fear.

Adventures in the Golden Canopy

Scaling up trees, what a sight to behold,
Golden laughter in piles, uncontrolled.
They hide from the sun, in shade they conspire,
Plotting their mischief, never to tire.

Swinging on branches, a merry brigade,
Creating a ruckus, their plans never fade.
With giggles and shouts, they scatter like seeds,
In a world full of fun, oh how it feeds!

Whimsical Tides of Bright Delight

An ocean of joy, in vibrant display,
Rolling on waves, they frolic and sway.
The tide whispers secrets, the sun's glowing face,
While fruity companions join in the race.

Splashing and playing, they surf on the foam,
In a world made for laughter, they're far from home.
With giggles fleeting, like bubbles in air,
Their venture continues, no hint of despair.

A Canvas of Gold and Azure

Yellow curves in the sun,
Chasing joy, just begun.
Birds take flight, what a prank,
Painting smiles on the plank.

Bouncing laughter all around,
Ticklish breezes, joy is found.
Playful whispers in the air,
Joyful shouts without a care.

A burst of cheer upon the tree,
Naughty giggles, set us free.
Fruitful mischief, oh so bright,
Dancing shadows in the light.

With every twist, a surprise,
Chasing dreams in sunny skies.
A bright chorus in the breeze,
Silly hats bring us to knees.

Skimming Clouds and Sweetness

Floating on a fluffy dream,
Giggles rise, a silly theme.
Tasty treats, oh what a scene,
Waving hats, a vibrant sheen.

Up above, a dance in flight,
Swirling joy, pure delight.
Sweetness drips from every smile,
Tripping laughter all the while.

Plucking joy from cotton fluff,
Every nibble, never tough.
Sunny chases all around,
With each drop, pure fun is found.

Swinging low, then soaring high,
Chasing clouds that drift on by.
In this realm of whimsy's flow,
Time stands still, and spirits glow.

The Laughter of Tropical Days

Beneath bright rays, we all unite,
Chasing each other, what a sight.
Sunny giggles, echo wide,
Tropical warmth as our guide.

Every bite bursts with delight,
Silly games from day to night.
Wipe away the solemn tears,
Joyful cheers erase our fears.

Rustling leaves, a gentle sound,
Life's sweet morsels all around.
With every breeze, a hearty laugh,
Painted smiles on each small path.

Coconut hats upon our heads,
Dancing while the sunlight spreads.
In this paradise of play,
Life's a joke — hip-hip-hooray!

Radiant Horizons and Fruity Whispers

Golden rays hug the land,
Playful antics, a merry band.
Sassy skies above do tease,
Bouncing fruit upon the breeze.

Whispers soft, like peanut butter,
Silly sounds that make you stutter.
Dip and dive in playful glee,
As the day calls out to me.

With every giggle, joy does swell,
Mischief brewed in nature's spell.
A splash of color, laughter loud,
Living moments that make us proud.

The call of laughter, bright and bold,
As the twilight's secrets unfold.
In every corner, vibrant cheer,
Life's delightful moments here.

Sun-Drenched Melodies of Life

In a land where laughter reigns,
Beneath the sun like playful stains.
Fruits giggle from their leafy nooks,
As sunbeams dance like happy books.

The birds compose a silly tune,
While clouds drift by like a silver swoon.
Every breeze tells a joke to share,
Laughter floats like perfume in the air.

With a cocktail of giggles on the side,
Joy bubbles over like a roller ride.
Each moment bursts with pure delight,
As we sway to the rhythm of light.

So come and frolic, don't be shy,
Let your worries flutter and fly.
In this paradise of merry play,
The sun be your guide, hip-hip-hooray!

A Tapestry Woven in Gold

Golden treasures hang with glee,
Weaving tales of jubilee.
Underneath the azure arch,
Every step feels like a march.

Chatter spills like nectar sweet,
With all the creatures keen to meet.
Nature winks from the branches high,
With every sigh, a joyful cry.

Woven laughter fills the air,
While critters dance without a care.
The sun tickles in playful jest,
Who knew life's tapestry could be the best?

So grab a friend and take a seat,
Join in the fun, oh what a feat!
Twirl and whirl in this grand parade,
In a world where joy is truly made!

Golden Fruits Beneath the Vast

Underneath the heavens bright,
Fruits are giggling, what a sight!
They sway gently on their strings,
Whispering tales of silly things.

A chubby squirrel starts to dance,
While bumblebees take a prance.
Every critter joins the song,
In this wacky place where we belong.

Vibrant colors spin and swirl,
Around the globe, watch laughter twirl.
Each moment's ripe with comic flair,
No reason left for a single care.

So let us feast on joy today,
In the warmth of the sun's bouquet.
With nature's jesters all around,
Life's sweetest laughter can be found!

Sweet Echoes of a Warm Embrace

Echoes bounce from tree to tree,
In a summer tune, wild and free.
Fruits chuckle on the vines so high,
Creating mischief as they pass by.

The sun's a jester, bright and bold,
Spreading warmth and stories untold.
With every step, the ground will sing,
As joy entwines in everything.

A gentle breeze, a tickling touch,
Reminds us all that laughter's such.
The air is thick with glee and cheer,
Inviting all who venture near.

So join the chorus, sing along,
In this land where we belong.
Amidst the giggles and the grace,
You'll find sweet echoes of a warm embrace!

Skimming Along Golden Shores

On sandy banks we start to play,
With smiles that shine throughout the day,
A slip and slide, we're free as birds,
With laughter loud, no need for words.

The sun above, a golden crown,
Roll on, roll off, we won't fall down,
In this sweet land, we're kings and queens,
Dancing on grains, oh what it means!

A frosty drink in hand we grasp,
With summer's kiss, a perfect rasp,
As waves tickle our toes so fine,
We revel in a world divine!

So bring the fun and never stop,
With wild antics, we all hop,
From beach to sun, a joyful song,
This carefree vibe is where we belong.

A Delicate Balance of Flavor and Light

A slice of joy upon my plate,
With creamy clouds, I celebrate,
A twist of zest and laughter bright,
This scrumptious treat, pure delight!

Adventures come with every bite,
Gold and sweetness take their flight,
I munch and crunch with cheerful flair,
Each taste a giggle, light as air!

Juggling fruit in the afternoon,
A comic dance, we sway and swoon,
With purple hues and yellow cheer,
My culinary dreams are here!

In this buffet of pure delight,
We laugh and munch from day to night,
With friends around, our spirits soar,
A grandeur feast—it's never a bore!

A Melody of Bright Adventures

Let's spin around in laughter's grace,
We whirl with joy—what a lovely race,
With chimes of giggles in our hearts,
A symphony where fun imparts!

A cartwheel here, a skip so free,
Through fields of dreams, just you and me,
The air is rich with sunny charms,
As we embrace all nature's arms!

We chase the clouds, pretend to fly,
With hands up high, we touch the sky,
Together we weave a vibrant tune,
Underneath the soft, sweet moon.

In every moment, joy collides,
With laughter echoing, hope abides,
A journey crafted, wild and bright,
As we compose our song of light!

The Taste of Luminous Joy

In morning's light, a treasure found,
With flavors bold, we sing aloud,
A hint of mischief on our lips,
In this sweet world, let's take our trips!

A splash of color on the scene,
With edible joy, oh so serene,
We giggle as we share our treats,
The sweetest moments, life repeats!

We plot and plan our food parade,
With sticky fingers, we won't fade,
Each crunchy bite, a clever prank,
A fruit-filled feast along the bank!

So take a bite, the taste of fun,
In every crunch, we're never done,
Together we savor, laugh, and cheer,
In this bright banquet, happiness is near!

A Journey Through Light and Taste

In a world where giggles float,
Fruit hats dance on every coat.
Yellow smiles on trees so tall,
Joyful whispers, come one, come all.

With every bite, a chuckle found,
Fragrance lifts, joy does abound.
Mirth weaves through the air so free,
Every flavor's a melody.

Underneath the warming glow,
Fruitful laughter starts to flow.
Chasing clouds with silly prance,
Life's a never-ending dance.

Every corner, bright delight,
Sweetness shines, oh what a sight!
With each moment, happiness grows,
Sunshine kisses, light bestows.

Sunshine's Gentle Hold on Us

In a land where giggles grow,
Laughter's warmth, a gentle glow.
Tickled toes on sunlit ground,
In this mirth, our joys are found.

Jumpy critters, silly stunts,
Nature's cheer, the wild haunts.
Swirling colors, bright and bold,
In each moment, laughter told.

Frolicsome tales of fruit and cheer,
In this sunshine, we hold dear.
Beneath clear skies, we stay so free,
Floating thoughts, wild jubilee.

Every shadow, a playful twist,
In this warmth, we can't resist.
With our hearts in gleeful flight,
Sunshine cradles us so tight.

The Enchantment of Vibrant Days

Magic lingers in the air,
Giggles bubble everywhere.
Twinkling toes on grass so green,
In a world that's never mean.

Colors burst like candy dreams,
Sweetness flows in sunshine beams.
Every moment, pure delight,
Chasing stars through day and night.

Fruity treasures on the ground,
In their glow, joy does abound.
Silly songs and dances flow,
Underneath the skies aglow.

Life's a laugh, a playful rhyme,
In this realm, we sway with time.
With a wink, the day is spun,
Happiness has just begun!

Dappled Light and Bright Delights

Golden rays through leaves cascade,
In this realm, sweet serenade.
Nonsense laughter fills the air,
Nature's stage, a grand affair.

With each tickle of the breeze,
Silly whispers dance with ease.
Chubby cheeks and giggle fits,
Painting joy in sunny bits.

Every moment's a new quest,
Where the curious find their best.
Bright stars peek through playful clouds,
In this magic, laughter shrouds.

Underneath the dappled shade,
Giggles linger, never fade.
In this bounty, life ignites,
With each heartbeat, pure delights.

The Dance of Warmth and Sky's Delight

In the garden where giggles play,
Fruits hang low in a cheerful sway,
Under sunshine's golden beam,
Joy bursts forth, a vibrant dream.

Laughter bubbles, a playful sound,
Chasing clouds that dance around,
With every peel, a smile grows wide,
In this world, fun takes a ride.

Splashes of color, a ticking clock,
Socks mismatched, we thinkers rock,
Nature's laughter fills the air,
Wobbly steps, without a care.

So grab a fruit, let's have a blast,
In this playground, joyful and vast,
Swing your arms, let spirits fly,
In light and joy, we dance and cry.

Kaleidoscopic Whimsy and Nature's Goodness

A twist of fate in stripes so bright,
Jesters dance in morning light,
With wobbly shoes and silly hats,
Here comes the parade of happy chats.

Lemonade rivers, sweet and cold,
Tales of mischief yet untold,
Nature's art in every bite,
Giggles echo, pure delight.

Round and round, we spin with glee,
Colorful dreams, come dance with me,
As petals flutter and whirl away,
We bask in joy, come what may.

Let's swing the worries, stretch and sway,
In the vibrant hues of the day,
With shades of laughter and cheer so bright,
The world is ours, what a grand sight!

Lush Delight Beneath An Expansive Palette

In twilight's glow, a daring cheer,
Fruits like treasures, oh-so-dear,
Beneath the arch of a cobalt dome,
We prance and play, our joyful home.

Rippling giggles sprinkle the day,
With jokers jiving in a fun array,
Grass tickles toes, the breeze a tease,
Each little moment brings us ease.

Let's twirl and tumble, let worries part,
Every chuckle is a work of art,
In nature's booth, we feast and laugh,
Together we craft our happy path.

Flip-flops flapping, hearts on fire,
We dance along with joy to inspire,
An explosion of colors, a feast for the eyes,
In our goofy paradise beneath sunny skies.

Golden Wonders and Heavenly Veils

With splashes of gold on this radiant land,
Wobbly fruits in a playful hand,
A carnival swell with every bite,
Whispers of sweetness, pure delight.

Cheerful shouts from a dappled crowd,
Mirthful spirits, all feeling proud,
Games of laughter filling the air,
A funny joke, if you dare.

Under the cloak of a popcorn sky,
Join in the dance, let worries fly,
With each jovial skip, we sway and spin,
In our joyful hearts, we always win.

So here's to mischief, to silly dreams,
Dancing and laughing, bursting at the seams,
Wrapped in happiness, let's spread the tales,
Of golden wonders and heavenly veils.

Cheerful Chimes in a Cerulean Realm

In a land where sunshine giggles wide,
Funky fruits in laughter abide.
Wiggly worms dance in the rays,
Making silly shapes, in a joyful maze.

Clouds roll by, wearing grins so bright,
Kites take flight, a whimsical sight.
Fruit stands bursting, a playful spree,
As bees buzz tunes in harmony.

Jellybean trees sway with delight,
While merry critters put on a fight.
Twinkling stars wink at the fun,
As daydreams frolic, on the run.

In this realm where giggles bloom,
The silly jester spreads the room.
With every chime, a chuckle's near,
In this vibrant world, all is clear.

Harvested Hues on a Canvas of Dreams

In gardens where oddities take root,
Peculiar shades replace the hoot.
Orange squiggles and purple skies,
Silly plants wear comical ties.

Watch the corn try to jive and sway,
The carrots march, a bright ballet.
Fruits with hats and boots on show,
Laughing as they steal the show.

Pies in fields, aroma so sweet,
Frogs in tuxedos dance on their feet.
Dandelions blow a playful tune,
Under the glance of a chuckling moon.

It's a carnival of colors, no doubt,
Where laughter and joy are all about.
Every harvest brings a comedic cheer,
Here's to the dreams that draw us near!

Nature's Canvas: Cheerful Yellows and Heaven's Blues

Under the azure, a jolly parade,
Frogs in tuxedos, a splashy crusade.
Sunflowers giggle, paintbrushes sway,
Tickling the clouds that drift light and gay.

Ants in large hats tugging a line,
Lemonade rivers, oh how they shine!
Squirrels debate who has the best tunes,
While raccoons sing under whimsical moons.

Every hue tells a story untold,
Of joyous moments and laughter bold.
Oh how the foliage dances with glee,
In this canvas where all hearts agree!

With nature's laughter splashed all around,
A circus of colors, in joy, we're bound.
So grab a paintbrush, let's make it bright,
In this world of fanciful delight.

Sounds of Laughter Amidst the Golden Tapestry

In fields of gold, the giggles play,
Wiggle worms take the lead today.
Flowers burst out in fits of cheer,
Tickling the toes of the butterflies near.

A quirky lilac hops down the lane,
Telling tales of joyful disdain.
While swaying dandelions join the fun,
Their fluffs exploding, setting the tone.

Frothy waves crash in a cheeky dance,
Fish wear sunglasses, in the sun they prance.
With laughter echoing off each shell,
In this sea of joy, all is well!

The tapestry glows in a vibrant array,
Where chuckles are woven, come what may.
So dip your toes in this joyous space,
And let every moment a smile embrace!

Delights of Dappled Sunlight and Skybound Grace

In a grove where laughter plays,
The fruit hangs low in sunny rays.
A cheeky squirrel does a dance,
Thinking it's found its grand romance.

With every twist, the shadows prance,
While breezes tease in leafy pants.
Joy rides high on curly vines,
Nature's giggles, pure, divine.

Colors burst like joyous cheers,
Tickled by whimsical, sunny spheres.
The laughter flows like bubbling streams,
In this place of wild, sweet dreams.

When skies play tricks and rainbows grin,
Nature's humor is a win-win.
The world draped in a vibrant coat,
Leaves us grinning, full of hope.

Vivid Joys on a Breeze of Tranquility.

A yellow splash against the blue,
Whispers laughter, bright and true.
Nuts and fruits in a humorous row,
Even the flowers start to glow.

Wobbling on a branch so fine,
A crew of critters sipping wine.
Each tip of a leaf, a playful tease,
As warm winds carry silly keys.

Skimming clouds, a lazy kite,
Dancing downward, what a sight!
The giggles echo in endless flight,
As butterflies join the joyful bite.

Nature laughs in hues so bright,
A stage where even shadows delight.
Each moment feels like a funny rhyme,
Basking in an endless time.

Sunshine in a Yellow Peel

A globe of cheer, all wrapped in gold,
Where tales of joy are daily told.
A slip upon the humor ride,
With giggles bursting, can't hide!

A troupe of jesters, dressed in bright,
Swings and twirls in dazzling light.
With peels that promise fun each day,
And laughter that just won't decay.

Cravings spark like sunny rays,
Hiccups follow in fruit-filled plays.
The trees sway with a knowing wink,
While bees buzz tunes, no time to think!

A splash of zest, a sweet delight,
In shadows cool, we say goodnight.
Chasing giggles on summer's breeze,
This sunny world begs us to seize.

Citrus Dreams Under Open Air

In a land where zesty dreams unfold,
The sun shines bright with tales of old.
Oh what fun, with summer's cheer,
Where fruity flings are always near.

Dancing leaves in a playful sway,
Sun-splash moments, bright as day.
The antics here are hard to beat,
A fruit parade on happy feet!

Clouds roll by with giggly grace,
Tickling the air in a funny chase.
With every swing, a burst of glee,
And laughter echoes, wild and free.

So gather round, let's share a toast,
To sunny moments we love the most.
With shadows stretching, hearts entwined,
In this banter, sweet peace we find.

A Day of Cheer in Nature's Palette

A fruit with spots, a slippery dance,
Giggles erupt with every chance.
A yellow jester swings so free,
Chasing clouds, what joy to see!

With laughter ripe upon the breeze,
Sunshine tickles 'neath the trees.
Each bite brings forth a silly grin,
Contagious joy that draws us in.

Nature's circus, oh what a show,
Bright colors splash, as breezes blow.
The world a canvas, absurd and bright,
Where even shadows seem to delight.

So gather round, take in the view,
Life is better when shared by two.
In nature's cheer, let's lose our cares,
And spin the tales that friendship shares!

Citrus Smiles Against a Sky of Wonder

Zesty orbs with a playful twist,
Wobble and nod, a citrus tryst.
Juicy laughter spills with light,
As clouds waltz, oh what a sight!

Each fruit, a giggle in disguise,
Cheerful antics that mesmerize.
The sunshine winks, a playful tease,
Inviting joy upon the breeze.

So let's parade beneath the sun,
With silly hats, this day is fun.
A zest for life, sweet and bold,
The stories here will never grow old.

Look up ahead, the skies are bright,
And every moment's sheer delight.
Together we'll dance, and swoop, and twirl,
In this blissful, fruity world!

The Brightness of Life in Every Shade

A cheerful splash of yellow cheer,
This fruity friend brings joy so near.
With soft giggles that softly sprout,
It giggles back; that's what it's about!

Each slice reveals a wacky grin,
While daring squirrels join in the spin.
The sunlight dances on the ground,
As laughter grows; it knows no bound.

A petal here, a laugh right there,
The world's a game of hide and share.
And if you trip on playful peels,
Just laugh it off; that's how joy feels!

So let's rejoice in colors bright,
With every prank, we share delight.
Beneath the sun, we're free to play,
In nature's fun, we'll find our way!

Overhead Wonder Complementing Earthly Joy

Above, the skies, a canvas wide,
With fluffy clouds that gently glide.
They whisper tales of wonder's cheer,
As laughter sparkles, drawing near.

Chasing breezes, we can't sit still,
With every fruit, the giggles thrill.
A splash of color, a silly hat,
What else is life but moments like that?

Each twist and turn brings silly glee,
Rolling around as wild as can be.
So let's create a story grand,
With goofy antics, hand in hand.

We'll chase the sun, embrace the round,
In joyfulness, our hearts unbound.
With every shade that brightens life,
We'll conquer the world, free from strife!

Threads of Joy in the Skies

In the trees, a yellow joke,
Swinging high, a fruity poke.
Laughter dances on the breeze,
Tickles toes and teases knees.

Clouds above are fluffy smiles,
Wandering free for miles and miles.
Light and laughter fill the air,
Silly thoughts without a care.

Bright peels strewn along the path,
Nature's giggle, full of glee and wrath.
Gusts sing tunes of sunny cheer,
While we munch—we're in the clear!

Joyful slips and little trips,
Fruitful fun with silly quips.
In this dance of sweet delight,
We bounce and twirl 'til the night.

Sunkissed Fruit of Life

Sunshine drips from leafy crowns,
Gather 'round, it's time for gown!
Tropical giggles bounce around,
As chubby cheeks, they do abound.

Juicy smiles in every bite,
Silly faces, pure delight.
Sticky fingers, laughter bright,
Days of play stretch out in light.

Clouds above like cotton candy,
Nature's candy makes us dandy.
With each chuckle, spirits soar,
Who knew fruit could mean much more?

Grins like suns that never wane,
With each snack, we lose the strain.
Let's frolic in this golden glow,
Crazy fruit, our hearts overflow!

The Lullaby of Warm Breezes

Whispers float through leaves so bright,
As silly critters dance in flight.
Swings of joy and gentle sighs,
Giggles rise to meet the skies.

From tree to tree, the laughter flies,
Bouncing 'round with goofy ties.
Warmth envelops, smiles abound,
In this feast of life, we're found.

Gentle rustles, playful calls,
As sunshine splashes, merriment sprawls.
Sweet aromas drift and sway,
Childlike wonder leads the way.

Breezes hum a tune so fine,
Tickling cheeks, oh how they shine!
In this moment, joy's embrace,
Dance and laugh in this bright space.

Heartfelt Whispers Under Sunbeams

Underneath the golden rays,
Joyous tricks ignite our days.
Silly tales that never tire,
Bouncing smiles lift us higher.

With every peal of radiant fruit,
We find our dance, to which we scoot.
Each little bounce, a jabbering cheer,
Echoes of laughter fill the sphere.

Little ones with gleeful grins,
Paint the world with playful wins.
Sweetness drips from every corner,
In this realm, all feels much warmer.

So let us play beneath this dome,
Each bright day, we find our home.
Whispers of joy, we won't forget,
In every bite, laughter's duet.

Whispers of Fruit and Clouds

In a garden bright and grand,
Where the yellow fruits all stand,
They giggle in the warm, soft breeze,
Tickling the branches, oh what a tease.

Fluffy clouds take shape and dance,
In a flurry of whimsical romance,
Fruits toss jokes from leafy heights,
While sunlight sparkles, igniting delights.

Silly squirrels prance about,
Munching treats, laughing with a shout,
Oh, how the colors spin and sway,
In this fruity, funny parade today!

Nature's laughter fills the air,
With every smile, every snatch of flair,
In this world where joy does bloom,
Who needs a recipe to make room?

Dancing in Joyful Hues

Underneath the sky so bright,
Grows a fruit that's pure delight,
Frolicsome leaves sway with glee,
Bouncing bright in harmony.

Puffy clouds in playful rings,
Join the dance, oh how it sings,
Twisting, twirling, all around,
Hidden treasures can be found.

Laughter echoes off the trees,
As a bird hops, flaps his keys,
Each branch holds a merry tune,
Nothing's gloom beneath this moon.

Smiles arise from every core,
With nibbles, giggles, and much more,
Life is a jolly, simple fare,
Beneath the sun's warm, golden glare.

The Tapestry of Morning Light

Awake the morning's vivid art,
As fruits flaunt their vibrant heart,
A jester's hat hangs on the vine,
Where laughter waits, how divine!

Fluffy clouds drift like a dream,
In a sunshine-kissed gleam,
All the colors blend and swirl,
With a wink and giggle, they twirl.

Jovial blossoms sway in cheer,
They're the whispers, oh so clear,
Beneath the sky that gently beams,
A playful dance of sweetened dreams.

Giddy breezes tease the day,
Sending silly thoughts at play,
Wrapped within this joyful flight,
Life's a canvas, pure delight!

A Feast of Sunshine and Air

Join the feast, it's quite the show,
Where ripened treats begin to glow,
Chubby cheeks and wide-eyed laughs,
Fill the air with silly crafts.

Clouds serve up a frosty drink,
While sunshine dances on the brink,
Fruits crack jokes, go on, have fun,
In this space where giggles run.

Delightful colors, purest cheer,
Fill the world, from far to near,
As melodies splash like a wave,
In this banquet, joy is brave!

So raise a toast to warmth and light,
With every bite, everything feels right,
For life's a feast, with laughter shared,
In nature's embrace, always cared!

Sunlit Slices of Happiness

In the garden, laughter grows,
With yellow smiles, a bright show.
Tiny peels tossed in the air,
Joyful giggles everywhere.

Jumps and twirls, a merry race,
Citrus dreams in sunlit space.
Sticky fingers and pure delight,
Chasing shadows, feeling light.

Everyone shares the sunny cheer,
With every munch, we spread good cheer.
A feast of fun, a vibrant day,
Where every worry fades away.

Golden treats and playful tunes,
Silly dances under moons.
Here we bask in sweet refrains,
Life's best treats, our funny gains.

A Sky Paved with Playfulness

Cotton clouds drift and sway,
Beneath them, kids laugh and play.
Air filled with snickers and yells,
As the sun casts its warm spells.

Silly hats and vibrant games,
The world is bright, no one blames.
In a field of giggles we soar,
Watch out for the muddy floor!

Chasing kites that twist and twirl,
Each step brings a playful whirl.
With every leap and funny face,
We write our dreams with joyful grace.

A splash of joy in every heart,
With every smile, we play our part.
Under the sun, we live so free,
In a world of laughs, just you and me.

Chasing the Warmth of the Day

With sunglasses perched atop our heads,
We dance around like tiny threads.
Melting ice cream drips and flows,
A sticky treat that everyone knows.

Laughter echoes through the park,
As chirping birds add their spark.
A game of tag, a race to win,
With every stumble, we'll grin again.

Bouncing on swings, reaching high,
Our worries float up to the sky.
A picnic spread with giggles galore,
Eating fruit, we always want more.

Growing tall like the flowers' cheer,
In this warm bubble, we hold dear.
Every moment, a joyful play,
We chase the bright warmth of the day.

The Essence of Summer's Embrace

Sunshine summons all to cheer,
We gather 'round with friends near.
A slip and slide, a splash of fun,
So much joy, we could run!

Chasing bikes down winding paths,
With every corner, endless laughs.
The smell of treats wafts through the air,
Silly stories and summer fare.

Picnic blankets laid out wide,
With pots of joy rolled side by side.
Silly hats upon our heads,
In this laughter, our hearts are fed.

Under the sun, we sing and sway,
In moments fleeting, we choose to stay.
The essence of joy wraps us tight,
In summer's embrace, everything's bright.

In the Heart of Sunlit Wonder

In the heart of bright delight,
Monkeys dance without a care,
Waving hats and jumping high,
Chasing dreams in sunlit air.

Lemon drops in cheeks they hold,
Jokes so loud, they make us grin,
With a splash, the laughter flows,
As silly games of tag begin.

Orange sunsets make us stare,
Tickled toes in sandy dew,
Every giggle fills the square,
Oh, what fun, and all's askew!

Bouncing balls and sliding feet,
Rolling laughter like a wave,
In this land of pure delight,
We'll be goofy, bold, and brave.

Glistening Smiles Under Radiance

Under skies that glow so bright,
Frogs in hats sing folk tunes free,
Chasing shadows, taking flight,
A carnival of mirthful glee.

Accordion cats strum their strings,
While wise owls offer guiding light,
All the universe just sings,
In our jests, the stars ignite.

Jellybeans in every hue,
Twirling 'round like confetti flies,
With a lucky charm or two,
We'll bask beneath the playful skies.

Jammin' songs and tasty treats,
In the breeze, the laughter flows,
We make magic with our beats,
Creating joy wherever goes.

The Sweetness of a Joyful Breeze

A soft refrain of silly songs,
Whistling through the fields so green,
With every note, our spirit throngs,
And transforms ordinary scenes.

Buzzy bees, they honk and cheer,
Dancing 'round in perfect sync,
Chasing butterflies so near,
As they sip on honey drink.

Frolicking through the sun-kissed air,
Balloons afloat like dreams untold,
Chasing smiles without a care,
Painting moments, bright and bold.

Every gust ignites delight,
Stories spun like golden thread,
Joyful laughter takes its flight,
In this land where fun is spread.

Waves of Gold Beneath Endless Blue

Waves roll in with foamy cheer,
Surfboards shaped like giant pies,
Splashing joy, no hint of fear,
Underneath the laughing skies.

Seagulls mimic silly songs,
With flapping wings and squawks galore,
Crafting rhythms, dancing throngs,
Call it magic on the shore.

Shells and treasures twist and twirl,
Every grain a secret shared,
While the ocean's playful swirl,
Pulls us in, forever dared.

As sunset casts its golden hue,
With sandcastles that rise and fall,
In our hearts, a dream come true,
Laughter echoes, joins the call.

Golden Curves Under Azure Horizons

In a grove where laughter plays,
Fruit in hand is what we praise.
Mischief in the air so sweet,
Chasing joy with dancing feet.

Under light that fills the day,
Silly pranks in bright display.
Swinging high on vines of glee,
Who knew fruit could set us free?

Ripe delights hang from the trees,
Tickling us with gentle breeze.
Sunshine smiles upon our quest,
Nature's jest, we love the best.

Giggling fruits, they roll and sway,
We chase their curves and laugh away.
In this land where fun will thrive,
Every moment feels alive!

Sun-Kissed Whispers in Fruity Hues

A splash of yellow in the sun,
Each giggle tells us life's a pun.
Jokes are shared with fruity flair,
   Joyful whispers fill the air.

Underneath this smiling glow,
We dance where sweet delights do grow.
Swinging high with friends we cheer,
   Life is fruity, full of cheer.

Silly faces, fruit so bright,
Twinkling eyes with sheer delight.
Joy rolls in on sunny rays,
   Fruity flavors, wild displays.

Every bounce, a burst of cheer,
Funny faces, bring it near.
Laughter echoes, wild and free,
   Come join us; it's pure glee!

Radiant Yellow Beneath Vast Ceilings

In a place where shadows fade,
Joyful moments are remade.
Wandering through fields so bold,
Stories in the sunshine told.

Golden hue, like playful dreams,
Bursting forth in radiant beams.
Laughter dances in our souls,
Fruity fun makes us feel whole.

Under skies of azure bright,
We leap and whirl with pure delight.
Silly hats and sunny shakes,
Brighten all our joyful wakes.

Soft whispers of a fruity breeze,
Telling tales that tease with ease.
Together, we create our space,
In this fun, we find our place!

Tropical Dreams and Celestial Canopies

Under swirling shades of bliss,
A twist of fate, a fruity kiss.
Puns abound like leaves in flight,
Here, we dance 'til falls the night.

Mirth and giggles fill the air,
With each fruit, a playful dare.
Bright adventures, surprise awaits,
As we feast on joy it creates.

In the shade of leafy trees,
We play around with lots of ease.
Funny tales take us away,
With fruity dreams that come to stay.

Lively laughter, warm embrace,
In this place, we find our race.
With every bite, a chuckle blooms,
In this land where whimsy looms.

A Toast to Golden Moments

In the land where fruit is bright,
Laughter dances in the light.
Peels are slipping, people grin,
Joyful chaos, let's begin!

Pies and smoothies fill the air,
With laughter as we sip our fare.
Golden snacks and silly cheers,
Chasing all our silly fears.

Juggling snacks, a wobbly feat,
Watch our clumsy little treat!
Fruits that bounce like bouncing balls,
We'll make memories in the halls.

So here's a laugh, let's raise a cup,
To all who love to mix it up!
With every squishy, juicy bite,
We find our joy in pure delight!

The Radiance of Nature's Palette

A splash of yellow, a dash of fun,
Nature's colors shine like the sun.
Splendid hues in every bite,
Sweet treats make our hearts feel light.

With giggles shared beneath the tree,
We plot adventures, wild and free.
Colorful bites that make us grin,
Let the fruity fun begin!

Whirls of laughter in the park,
Chasing pips till it gets dark.
Nature's gifts, so sweet, so bold,
Beneath the sky, our tales unfold.

So grab a friend, and grab a snack,
Dance in flavors, never look back!
With sunlight shimmering on our cheek,
We celebrate the joy we seek!

Beneath the Shade of Sunlit Dreams

Here we lie in sunny glee,
Underneath the wise old tree.
Fruity fun in the gentle breeze,
A world of giggles, oh, please!

Peels that fly like paper planes,
Laughter spills, we're off the chains.
Sun-kissed snacks, a joyful mess,
Happiest days, what more, I guess?

Shady spots where whispers bloom,
Stories gathered 'round this room.
Eating treats with zestful flair,
Golden bites beyond compare!

Let's toast to all the silly times,
Where laughter flows like nursery rhymes.
Beneath the shade, our dreams take flight,
Savor every silly bite!

A Whirl of Flavor and Color

Round and round the laughter swirls,
Fruity treats for all the girls.
Colors bright, they pop and dance,
Who could ever miss this chance?

With every scoop and every slice,
Life's a treat, and oh, so nice!
Giggles echo through the air,
Every snack, a priceless share.

Here we spin and twirl with glee,
Creating moments, wild and free.
Taste the joy, feel the delight,
Flavor bursts, oh what a sight!

So let's embrace this goofy spree,
In joy-filled days, just you and me.
With vibrant flavors, laughter high,
We celebrate beneath the sky!

Sunshine Serenade in a Yellow Grove

In a grove where laughter spills,
Yellow fruits with happy thrills,
Swaying trees in playful dance,
Nature's charm, a bright romance.

Squirrels leap with gentle grace,
Chasing shadows, quicken pace,
A peal of joy, a sunny shout,
What a world, without a doubt!

Leaves are giggling, birds are loud,
Sunshine blankets every crowd,
Fruitful dreams that make you smile,
Let's enjoy this quirky style!

Dancing in the light so clear,
Snack attacks bring us good cheer,
With each slice and every bite,
Life is sweet, and all feels right.

Azure Elegance with a Hint of Sweetness

Bright blue skies, a canvas wide,
Sweetest treats, our joy can't hide,
Golden mounds in playful heaps,
Nature's bounty, laughter leaps.

Breezes whisper silly tales,
Wiggly worms in sunny trails,
Chasing giggles, chasing dreams,
Life's a party bursting at the seams!

Clouds are fluff, like cotton candy,
Dancing moods, not too randy,
Fruitful fun in azure bliss,
Don't you dare dismiss this!

With a wink and playful cheer,
Sweets abound, it's crystal clear,
Nature's smile, a jolly treat,
Good vibes come, where fun's complete!

Curved Radiance in the Morning Light

Morning beams in gentle arcs,
Silly jokes, and playful sparks,
Golden curves in bright array,
Life's a hoot, come join the fray!

Chasing shadows, jumping high,
Picnic spreads in open sky,
Fruit so bright, a vibrant tease,
Joyful moments aim to please!

Giggling winds, they swirl about,
Dancing leaves begin to shout,
A party hat upon a tree,
What a sight, wouldn't you agree?

Sips of nectar, every sip,
Laughter flows and makes us flip,
With each dawn, a brand new chance,
To laugh and play, let's take a stance!

Blissful Harvest Beneath Endless Blue

In fields of gold, we laugh and play,
Harvest joys in bright array,
Smiles abound, so sweet and round,
In this paradise, cheer is found.

Pigs in mud and frogs that croak,
Nature's stage is such a joke,
Ripe delights hang from each branch,
Let's all sing and do a dance!

Bubbles rise in sunlight's gleam,
Joyful hearts embrace the dream,
With a twist and playful grin,
We chase the light, let fun begin!

Under skies that never fade,
Every moment's a charade,
With friends who brighten up the night,
Every chuckle feels so right!

www.ingramcontent.com/pod-product-compliance
Lightning Source LLC
Chambersburg PA
CBHW070004300426
43661CB00141B/219